Barry Manilow

BARRY MANILOW

by
Mark Bego

Edited by Barbara Williams Prabhu

Tempo Books
Grosset & Dunlap
A Filmways Company
New York, N.Y.

1

The Music Maker

"**I**'m just a musician who sings a little." That's how Barry Manilow, America's top recording artist, has summed up his fantastic career!

Just five short years ago, the good-looking blond from Brooklyn, New York, was an unknown piano player. Today, at thirty-two, the six-foot-tall dynamo is a *music master* due to his extraordinary talents as a singer, songwriter, arranger, pianist, and performer. The excellence and vast appeal of his recordings have kept his name on the national music charts for more than three years.

Beginning with the release of the song "Mandy" in the fall of 1974, each of Barry's single records has become a chart-topper. Since "Mandy" became number one, Manilow songs such as "Could It Be Magic?" "I Write the Songs," "I Think We Made It," and "Tryin' to Get the Feeling," have made Barry one of the country's top box-office draws.

With one gold and four platinum albums to his credit, Barry Manilow is riding high on an unbeatable winning streak. During the spring and summer of 1977 he had the rare distinction of having five long-playing albums appearing on the *Billboard* magazine charts at the same time! Only Frank Sinatra and Johnny Mathis have previously accomplished this feat!

From July 1976 through April 1977 Barry, his backup trio "Lady Flash," and his band City Rhythm, performed in ninety-eight cities across the country. The Christmas engagement of the tour was a two-week booking on

Broadway at the Uris Theater. The 1,900-seat theater was sold out well in advance of the holidays.

Barry's fifth long-playing album entitled *Barry Manilow Live,* released a month after the tour was completed, is a collection of tapes gathered during the Christmas 1976 stage show. The album was certified platinum by the Record Industry Association of America for sales of 1 million records, and the following summer became number one in the country.

On March 2, 1977, ABC-TV broadcast the first "Barry Manilow Special." The show was seen by over 35 million people and received the 1977 Emmy for Best Musical Variety Show.

Twice the Grammy Awards Record of the Year nominee, Barry was honored with a "special" Tony Award on June 6, 1977, for his Christmas 1976 performance. Three months later his televised special received the Emmy.

For all his success, Barry has remained a sincere, good-natured person,

Rehearsing for the engagement at the Uris
Theater in 1976. *UPI*

Barry with Lady Flash. *Photo by Bob Scott*

yet very much his own man. "I have a
wall full of gold records . . . and that's
my reward. I'm happy. But, it's a life of
hard work," Barry has said. "I'm not
sociable because I choose not to be. I'm
much too busy with my work, first of

all. Besides, I don't like parties. I don't like being phony, and I'm not good at small talk."

Barry's main professional intent has always been to lead the listening audience back to what he calls "intelligent music." According to this very sincere young man, "I'm trying to bring back intelligent music; in contrast to noise, in contrast to distortion. Just go get a little more complex, a little more complicated musically and lyrically, a little deeper."

Today he is an acknowledged media "star." But the fanfare of show business isn't what makes Barry Manilow happy.

"My first love is being a musician and that's where I'm most comfortable. Getting out there in my glitter clothes, and talking and carrying on, it's part of what I do, but it's not really the most of it. The most fun I have is when I'm in the studio, and when I'm working with a whole bunch of musicians."

Today Barry is on both sides of the

fence, trading hats between the roles of "singer" and "arranger." As he explains it, "It's a definite advantage, but not an absolute necessity." Much of Barry's self-taught professionalism was picked up during the early 1970s when he was writing and arranging music; at the same time he was playing piano in New York clubs and doing a bit of singing as well. Many critics and reviewers have commented on Barry's sophistication, his polished performances. The young man in his early twenties was learning the music business from the inside out—he was, and is, into every facet of musical production.

As his longtime friend, drummer and photographer Lee Gurst has said, "Barry coproduces his recordings, because he can't be in two places at once. He's got to have another pair of hands and ears to help, but I think Barry hasn't gotten enough credit for the work he's done. He wrote the last [television] special, he conceived the last special, he directed four-fifths of the last special. The choreography that was done on the last special was done by Lady Flash and Barry Manilow. Barry Manilow is a Barry Manilow production, not all the people who put their names on these products!"

Yes, Barry has put an incredible amount of energy into perfecting each facet of his chosen craft—and his achievements have been recognized and rewarded by the entire pop music industry.

In five short years, Barry Manilow has come a very long way from the Williamsburg section of Brooklyn, where it all began.

2

The Early Years

Barry Manilow was born in Brooklyn, New York, on June 17, 1946. An only child, he lived with his mother and grandparents in the not-too-attractive Williamsburg section of Brooklyn. His father deserted the family when Barry was two, and Barry's memories of his childhood are very vivid.

"I come from Division Avenue in Williamsburg—oh, it's so painful! Roots are really the strangest thing to talk about. I'm a definite slum kid; but though I got beaten up a lot by the kids on the block, I lived in a very nice house, and I was treated terrifically by my parents and grandparents, and I never knew I was a slum kid."

Barry tells of his second birthday when his Grandpa, Joe Manilow, took him to Times Square where they went into one of those old coin-operated "Make-a-Record" machines found in amusement arcades. Grandpa Joe's words are captured on the scratchy waxing as he prodded microphone-shy Barry: "Sing it . . . sing 'Happy Birthday' . . . Don't you want to make a record? . . ." That same waxy recording from Times Square, on which Barry utters only a handful of syllables, opens side one of the album *Barry Manilow I*.

"I was into music when I was a kid," Barry remembers. "It was the Andrews Sisters when I was three years old, with my mother bopping around the house."

Manilow recalls his old neighborhood gang: "We kids listened to rock and roll on the candy store jukebox and harmonized on street corners." At the

Photo by Shaun Considine - Globe Photos

age of seven he began taking accordion lessons.

"When I was thirteen years old my stepfather introduced me to 'intelligent' music by taking me to a Gerry Mulligan-

Art Farmer concert. I still remember that concert as if it were yesterday." Barry's early favorites were drawn from the jazz world and that first concert at Town Hall left a lasting impression on him.

Barry recalls his upbringing as being very practical. "I was raised to get a job and collect that paycheck every week, but even if I couldn't be doing what I'm doing now, I'd still be in music somehow even if I had to sweep floors in a recording studio.

"When it came time to decide what I was going to do with my life, I knew music was going to be a part, but I didn't want to take the gamble of actually deciding to make music my living. I could not believe, first of all, that it could be done. Secondly, that I could do it. I thought I would starve in a matter of months. So, I decided to go to City College [of New York] for advertising and still play music on weekends. I got so bored learning about marketing, merchandising, and textiles, that I finally told myself, 'Aw, come on an' give music a try.' "

Barry then attended the New York College of Music and later transferred to The Juilliard School of Music where he spent two semesters.

As the jazz influence on popular music changed, so did Barry's tastes. "Then rock and roll began to creep in. But for awhile, I never paid much attention to it. I really didn't like 'Rock Around the Clock.'

"I think the Beatles finally convinced me there was something going on in rock. I said, 'Hold it, would you run that by me again?' After that rock got better—better than the same old four chords, which never really turned me on. And Laura Nyro's *Eli* album—that was a great influence on my songwriting."

When Barry was asked if there was some sort of system or technique connected with his songwriting, he said: "Ask any songwriter and you get another answer. There's no system to

14

writing a song. Sometimes the lyrics come first; sometimes the music. It depends. It's impossible to describe. All I knew at the time I began writing was that many performers didn't seem to be saying enough. And too often the lyrics didn't fit the music. I wasn't moved by many performers. Arrangers inspired me more. But, I must admit, the Beatles began to get to me."

While Barry completed his studies, a job working in the CBS mailroom helped to pay the rent and put him in touch with some significant contacts. The first was Linda Allen who is now his general manager and constant companion. Linda was working in the programming department at CBS and gave him an opportunity to arrange some new music for the theme of the local station's "Late Show."

Another contact was a director who asked eighteen-year-old Manilow to do some arrangements for a production of his. This led to work on a musical version of the stage play "The

Drunkard." Barry began by arranging some public domain songs for it, that is, songs that are no longer under copyright protection. By the time his task was finished, he had written a score and inserted additional original material. The play ran for six years Off-Off Broadway, and for two years Off Broadway.

It was about this time that Lee Gurst entered Barry's life. As Lee tells it: "I went to New York to go to college and was hired to do an Off-Broadway show for which Barry Manilow was the musical director. It was a thing called *Now*, an ill-fated little musical at the Cherry Lane Theater, and Barry was the piano player, and I was the drummer. We had a guitar player, and we were the band. And so, we got along very nicely, we liked working together, we hit it off well, and began a string of jobs. . . ."

Barry had left the CBS mailroom for six months to pursue a show business career, but ended up back at

Barry accepts his award. *Photoreporters, Inc.*

CBS one more time before devoting all of his energies to music. This opportunity came when Barry was invited to become musical director of a weekly series "Callback" that showcased young talent. It was on the air for two seasons and won an Emmy citation. Barry was finally out of the mailroom—for good this time!

Perhaps because of his exposure on "Callback" Barry's musical career was picking up. "Then I got a call from the Ed Sullivan people, asking me to be music director for a series of new pilots they were doing after the Sullivan show went off the air. That was my big network conducting debut."

As Barry tells it: "I had become pretty good. I really worked at arranging and playing for singers, and I was able to get a lot of work. I was making a decent living and I loved it. I was accompanying just about every singer in town, in clubs and for auditions, for fifteen bucks an hour."

According to Barry, there are

Barry with his agent and friend Linda Allen.
Photo by Steve Schapiro - Sygma

important differences between singer
and arranger. "For a singer, it's not
difficult to learn a new arrangement
just from hearing it a couple of times,
memorizing it; he or she wouldn't have
to know how to read music. For an

Barry with Donny Most of TV's "Happy Days." *Photo by Irv Steinberg - Globe Photos*

arranger, though, it's important to understand all the possibilities of every instrument you're dealing with and know how to write music too. It would be hard to arrange without knowing how to write and read music, but I suppose it could be done."

While coaching and arranging for singers, Barry wrote a song that one of the vocalists recorded on a demonstration tape. The singer then took the tape around to a number of commercial agencies in the hope of landing work singing in advertisements. Not only did the agencies like the singer, but they also asked where the song came from. "He gave the agency my number," Barry recalls, "and they called me. And . . . I started working for them as a writer, and finally a singer.

"Basically I had a pretty hot streak, on commercials, as a writer and as a singer. By that time I decided that I enjoyed singing and I also decided that you made more money from singing commercials than you do from writing them. So, it was a combination of writing, arranging, and singing jingles from one to the other, or all three. They would hire me to do either one . . . .

"In the beginning there was one

[agency], but near the end of them . . . you see I don't do commercials anymore; I just have no time . . . but before I started going on the road, it was about five different agencies."

This was the beginning of Barry's transition from conducting, arranging, and accompanying to writing, performing, and recording his own compositions. "It was better than playing in bars," he recalls.

Since Barry's become a star, there's been lots of confusion as to which commercials were and were not written and/or sung by him.

Among his best-known commercials are *Kentucky Fried Chicken, Jack-in-the-Box,* and *McDonald's* (sang original versions); *Dr. Pepper* and *Pepsi* (sang someone else's compositions); *Bowlene Toilet Cleaner* and *Band-Aids* (wrote and arranged); *State Farm Insurance* (wrote); *Stridex* (wrote and sang) and *Chevrolet* (wrote, sang, *and* arranged).

A medley of Barry's better-known

Partying with Roberta Flack at the St. Regis
Hotel. *Wide World Photos*

jingles still draws a fantastic response in his live performances, and is showcased as Barry's "Very Strange Medley."

Elaborating on the commercials era, Lee Gurst explains, "I was involved only as a musician. Barry was coaching a number of singers and playing auditions for a lot of people, and beginning to write some songs. It came time to go in and do a couple of demos for his things, and singing on his demos . . . and a few other things.

"I think one of the earliest was . . . there were a couple of bank commercials in Pennsylvania, and a couple of tries at a Dodge Charger, which was not bought. They were submitted to the agency, they requested them, and they used the bank commercials in Pennsylvania. One led to another, and after writing a couple, then he began to play piano on them, and then to sing on a couple of them. All of a suddden, when his records began to go, it was 'Let's get Barry Manilow to do a Kodak commercial!' or something like that. . . ."

Barry's talents were getting lots of exposure, and just about the time when it was right for him to record one of his own songs, along came Irv Biegel, formerly with Bell Records, now vice-president of Millinium Records. Irv was the man who first signed Barry to a solo recording contract.

Having seen Barry on a couple of occasions, Irv Biegel recognized some of his yet-unexplored capabilities. According to Irv, Barry was part of a group called "Featherbed." Bell Records signed the group to a one-record deal, a single, about which Irv has said "Don't ask me the name of the song, because we didn't sell three copies." But on the "B" side of the single was a song titled "Could It Be Magic?" with music and lyrics by Barry, Adrienne Anderson, and F. Chopin. The record was produced by Tony Orlando. Lee Gurst has revealed that Barry wasn't *with* the group Featherbed—he *was* the group!

A smiling Eyde Gorme gives Barry a well deserved award. *Photo by Nate Cutler - Globe Photos*

According to Gurst, "In those days it was not common for singer/song-writers to be releasing a lot of things under their own name. A great many groups that have recorded through the years have been one individual. The Archies, the Cufflinks, the Detergents ... were all Ron Dante! All of them ... at the same time!"

As Irv Biegel has put it, "Al! right, so now Featherbed comes along and nothing happens ..." There's not much that can be said when a record doesn't make it. But in connection with Barry's first attempt to record one of his own compositions, two important things can be said. First, that the "B" side "Could It Be Magic?" was a sleeper that would awaken later in Barry's career, bringing the magic of fame and fortune. The second thing is that although few of the people involved knew it, this was a turning point in Barry's career, a giant step that would eventually lead him to the very pinnacle of show business.

CHAPTER

3

Music, Music, Music

It was in the spring of 1972. Barry Manilow was a very busy twenty-six year old—coaching singers, playing backup at auditions, arranging, writing, and singing commercials, and in his spare time (!) composing and singing his own material. But, for all his activity, Barry lacked exposure. He was known to a limited number of people and he knew that to grow he had to reach out to the public, so he continued to play the clubs.

Barry took a job as a piano player in New York's Continental Baths. Two weeks later, in walked Bette Midler, ready to be discovered by the world!

"It was hate at first sight,"recalls Barry, "but we rehearsed anyway. And Saturday night came, and there I was at the Continental Baths in a roomful of naked men and towels, and Bette came on stage looking like my mother with a fox around her neck and a turban on her head. I was rolling under the piano!"

When Barry first checked into the Continental Baths he figured he was getting a bit more exposure—mixing it up with the public. But, in no time, he became Bette's pianist, arranger, and producer, and the partnership lasted for two years!

Lee Gurst recalls that Barry was very, very enthusiastic about working with Bette. "He wanted me to work with her, but she already had her own group, so that didn't work out. And when they needed someone and hired me as a replacement for a sub, I started

Barry is at the piano in 1972 as Bette Midler's pianist and music arranger. *Photo by Bob Deutsch*

working with her. So I was around for that. It was an interesting experience... wandering into the path of someone like Bette Midler!

"Barry was very impressed with her. I found him devoting a lot of time

and energy to coaching her and working with her ... developing an act. I think he saw something really worth being involved with, and worth building and developing . . . ."

Working with Bette, Barry got more

exposure than he had expected, and made friends and contacts along the way.

Don Kirshner, host/producer of TV's popular weekly "Don Kirshner's Rock Concert" and annual "Rock Awards," remembers that Ron Dante, one of Kirshner's staff producers and a close friend of Barry's, brought him to the Midler opening at the Continental Baths. "Ron always used to talk about Barry Manilow," Don recalls. "And, when Bette Midler opened, I went with Ronny and his wife to see her, and Barry was conducting in the background.

"Ron brought Barry in one day, and Barry proceeded to play me two or three songs . . . which I thought were O.K. I was about to sign Barry as a writer, but his deal was too tough; he wanted half of the publishing rights. This was at the time he was doing commercials, and I knew him from the streets with all of the other kids.

"I said, 'We can't make a deal,' and

eventually he signed with Clive Davis and Arista Records. But, what was interesting inside of that . . . we stayed friendly."

Irv Biegel also remembers these early days in Barry's career, but for slightly different reasons. "Barry comes back, and he's playing piano for Bette. He comes back in with an almost-complete master called 'Sweetwater Jones.' He comes in with Ron Dante, whom I knew much better than I knew Barry. And they play me three sides that were not totally finished, and I fall in love with it! So I make a one-record deal with them, with the option for an album. 'Sweetwater Jones' comes out— and nothing happens . . ."

Barry has explained: " 'Sweetwater Jones,' that was the single release. It got picked up in Philadelphia, but it's hard. I had never done anything; they couldn't even pronounce my name, why should they play the record!? You know; so it never really happened, but it was strange."

Bette and her newly formed act found itself in immediate demand. First they finished up at the Baths, then there was an engagement at Upstairs at the Downstairs—then a recording contract for Bette, which meant more exposure and more studio experience for Barry.

What came out of Bette Midler's contract with the Atlantic Recording Studios was a classic album entitled *The Divine Miss M*. Released in December 1972, it was soon certified gold for sales of 500,000 copies, and later nominated for a Grammy Award. The album established Bette as a nationally known sensation and was a fabulous credit for the talented performers who contributed to the "divine disc."

On "Do You Want to Dance?" Barry does a rhythm track and is featured on piano. Ralph MacDonald does percussion work and a string and horn section, and Cissy Houston is among the backup vocalists. Barry also does a rhythm track and plays piano on "Friends," and "Am I Blue."

The production credits were shared by Barry, Geoffrey Haslam, and Ahmet Ertegun on "Chapel of Love," "Superstar," "Daytime Hustler," "Leader of the Pack," "Delta Dawn," and the concluding version of "Friends." On those six songs, Miss M's rhythm section is Barry Manilow, piano; Dickie Frank, guitar; Michael Federal, bass; Kevin Ellman, drums. Miss M's backup vocal group, the Harlettes, is comprised of Gail Kantor, Merle Miller, and Melissa Manchester.

By the fall of 1973, Bette had become the fastest rising star of the 1970s, and Barry, who had just released his own debut album *Barry Manilow*, was right there with her! Bette was invited to take the show on a four-month national tour that would include thirty-five cities.

Before Barry agreed to go on the tour, he made Bette's concert promoters a proposition. "I wouldn't go out on

Bette's tour unless they let me do my number!" he said. And *they* said, "Sing in the middle of a Bette Midler act! Are you nuts?" He may have been "nuts," but he got his way, and Barry did his bit—two or three of his own compositions—at the beginning of the second half of Bette's show, a slot he refers to as "the middle of World War II."

"The first gig I did my number with Bette was in front of 8,000 people in Columbia, Maryland, after she had driven them crazy in the first act. I was sitting at the piano conducting 'Do You Want to Dance?' and I knew, as I finished the last note, with people screaming and yelling as Bette walked off, that after the intermission the first one they were going to see was me. I wasn't on the bill; I was just listed as music director. So nobody knew I was going to come out and sing three of my original songs in the middle of bedlam. It was outdoors and you could not see the end of the people—just thousands of heads. So what did I do? What any

With Melissa Manchester. *Photo by Irv Steinberg - Globe Photos*

other redblooded American boy would do—I threw up!

"But it worked. I can't figure out why!

"We played the Red Rock Amphitheater in Colorado, a theater carved right into this mountain, with only the

Aiming to repeat his success in the States, Barry went to Britain in 1976. *Syndication International - Photo Trends*

mountain as backdrop. I sang 'Could It Be Magic?' and they went bananas— even with this long Chopin prelude and its being so different from Bette's act. That was my first standing ovation ever."

They toured the country, with Barry opening the second half of the show. For the first time in his career he was performing alone—and the crowds loved him! While on the road, Barry worked hard to perfect his performance, and his efforts were rewarded by the audiences' responses.

During the four months of the tour, the *Barry Manilow* album (the "I" at the end was added later) sold 35,000 copies. One month before the tour ended in December 1973, Bette's second Atlantic album *Bette Midler* was released. It soon hit the top twenty on the charts, and was certified gold. The album showed off Bette's vast talent, and paved her way to the wind-up engagement of the tour—three sold-out weeks at New York's Palace Theater. Bette and Barry were greeted with cheering ovations and saluted by encore demands.

Those final weeks of the Midler tour were very hectic for both Bette and Barry.

The sixteenth annual Grammy Award nominations were announced, and Bette was named in two categories, as Best New Artist and *The Divine Miss M* for Album of the Year. The recording artists as well as the producers of the album (including Barry) were listed under the nominees.

When the awards were actually presented in February 1974, Stevie Wonder's *Innervisions,* captured the coveted prize for Album of the Year, and Bette took Best New Artist award. Although Barry didn't get an award, he did get a taste of the Grammy nominations and the awards presenta-

In the recording studio. *Photo by Steve Schapiro - Sygma*

tion. He didn't know it then, but it wouldn't be long before *his* name would be nominated as a headline performer.

It was during this period that Barry made what Irv Biegel has called "one of the best moves he's ever made in his career." According to Irv: "He brings in a gentleman named Miles Lourie who was acting as his lawyer, but now becomes his manager.

"And, I think ... the success ... a lot has to be attributed to Miles Lourie. The way Barry's career was handled: with kid gloves!"

Irv claims to have fallen in love with the Midler/Manilow show in Jacksonville, Florida. "And I come back and they're finishing the tour in New York. It's even better, because the more he's out, the better he is."

At the end of their three weeks at the Palace, Bette went on a year's vacation to recover from total exhaustion. She'd gone from the Continental Baths on West 74th Street to Broadway's Palace Theater on West 47th Street in less than two years. Although it was only a matter of twenty-seven blocks, she had to cross the country twice, working hard each time she got onstage. The audience knew she gave her all, and they loved her for it.

As the new year began, Bette, her backup group the Harlettes, her band, and her arranger-conductor-pianist-friend, were all out on their own.

January 1974 was a time for new beginnings, especially for Barry Manilow.

4
Mandy

"A lot of people think I left Bette willingly," Barry has said. "It wasn't that at all. After the tour, she simply stopped working to take a long rest. There was no choice about it. Looking back, though, I guess it was good it happened."

Barry spent the beginning of 1974 assembling his own act. Bette's Harlettes were also out of work, so Barry adopted them and readied himself for a tour and further promotion on his first album, *Barry Manilow*.

Barry knew that the transition from

doing a couple of numbers in the middle of Bette's show, or recording in a studio, to performing up front before thousands of people, would be a big step. He's said the transition wasn't solely his idea. "I was thrown from behind the piano! Because, at the time Arista was Bell Records, and they wouldn't give me a record deal, unless I promised I would go out and perform, and I didn't really want to go out and perform, but I did want to make records, because I really loved being in the studio.

"So, I put an act together; you know I think I know how to do that . . . I've been doing that for about ten years, and coaching people. . . .

"So, we put it together, and it came out real strong, and it gave me a foundation to be able to make mistakes as a performer, because the basis was so strong, the music and the girls singing and the band. . . . I didn't want to give the whole burden to me because I'd never done it before, and yet here I was headlining in Philadelphia, and headlining all over the place. . . .

"Little by little, I got into it. Now I really enjoy it; I really enjoy performing! . . . I like the music, and I like making the music, and I like the audience reacting, because I'm doing it for them! So, it's a nice trip!"

Before taking the show on the road, however, a mammoth dress rehearsal was put on at Carroll's Rehearsal Studios. People from the industry, and from the press, as well as friends and executives of Bell Records, were invited to the preview. Lee Gurst has said it was a "show-off rehearsal," but it pleased a lot of people who were unaware of the full magnitude of Barry's accomplishments. And Bell Records picked up on their option for an album that they had negotiated with the single "Sweetwater Jones."

Through all of these experiences, Barry was amassing quite a winning team of people behind him. He was gaining confidence both onstage and

off, based on his knowledge that the behind-the-scenes details were run smoothly. Heaviest on the team were, and are, Miles Lourie, his manager; Ron Dante, his coproducer; and a newcomer at this point in Manilow's career, Clive Davis, his record company's president.

An amazing figure in the recording industry, Clive Davis is a born survivor. After establishing himself with Bell Records in 1974 he changed the company name to Arista Records and dumped all of its artists; with the exception of Barry, Melissa Manchester, and the Bay City Rollers. As proof of his business knowhow, in less than four years Arista has grown to one of the largest recording labels in the music industry.

Barry's first solo tour began in Boston. He wasn't yet a household word but audiences soon discovered he was in town. That first night in Boston at Paul's Mall, Barry did his thing before thirty-five to forty people! The next night there were 200 in the audience, and from there it got better. As Irv Biegel has said "Every place he went, people just got excited! Absolutely!" From Boston the show went on to Philadelphia, then to Memphis. Barry was reaching out to the public.

After six months on the road, Barry, the Harlettes, the band, and the backup people returned to New York.

Barry recalls a very special meeting he had with Clive Davis after the tour was over. "Clive showed me 'Mandy'—'Brandy,' as it was called originally," Barry remembers of the Scott English/Richard Kerr composition. "First we changed the name to 'Mandy.' I went into the studio to record it and Clive came down and sat next to the piano. . . ." When the recording session was completed, Clive said, 'Oh, it's wonderful, wonderful! Barry, if you have a hit with this ballad, your career is made?' "

Both the single "Mandy" and Barry's second L.P. *Barry Manilow II*

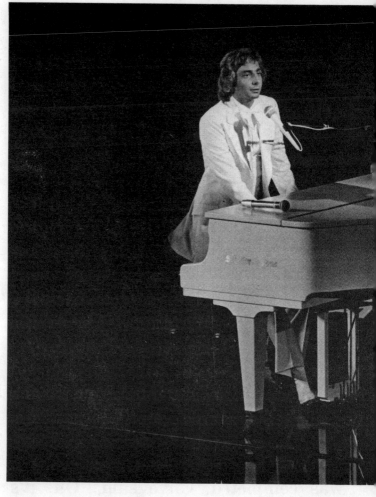

were released in the fall of 1974. Right away "Mandy" hit the charts. "The minute people played it," Barry recalls, "it went faster than anything! I hadn't

been involved with anything other than Bette's career. I had never seen a record go like that, in my life! That record was jumping twenty, thirty points a week, and it went number one in five, six weeks.

"All of a sudden, it was just all over. I couldn't turn the radio on without hearing it, and we'd just released it!" Eight months after Barry's first solo performance, "Mandy" was number one in the country.

The album *Barry Manilow II* was produced by Barry and Ron Dante at The Hit Factory and at Media Sound Studios. With four different lyricists, Barry wrote seven of the ten songs included.

Among the album cuts is a Motown classic, written by William Stevenson, Sylvia Moy, and Ivy Hunter, and originally made a hit by Martha Reeves and the Vandellas called "My Baby Loves Me." Barry's version gives a new melodic interpretation to the lyrics.

In the midst of all this recording activity, Barry headlined a concert at Carnegie Hall on November 12, 1974. He brought down the house with a Martha Reeves and the Vandellas medley. The concert, like the album, drew rave reviews.

By January 1975, "Mandy" was number one on the charts and was certified gold. The same month Barry released another single, "It's a Miracle," that also shot up to the top of the charts! It almost seemed that Barry could do no wrong, at least musically!

Ever the perfectionist, Barry now began to have second thoughts about the quality of some of the cuts on his first album, *Barry Manilow*. In April, he brought his backup singers (known as The Flashy Ladies) and his band (City Rhythm) into Media Sound Studios in New York and remixed four of the tracks of the original album, specifically, "One of These Days," "Oh My Lady," "Sweet Life," and "Could It Be Magic?" The new version was released in June 1975 as *Barry Manilow I* at the same time "Could It Be Magic?" was released as a single.

Regarding the remixing of that first album, Barry has said, "Yes, I had a chance to say, 'If I could have done it again, I would have done this.'"

While "Could It Be Magic?" was busy climbing its way to gold status, Barry was back in the studio working on yet another album: *Tryin' To Get The Feeling*. Recorded during the summer of 1975, it was released in October, was certified gold four weeks later, and like *Barry Manilow I*, eventually went platinum. The single "I Write the Songs," written by Bruce Johnson, was released at the same time. By January 1976 it was number one on the charts and certified gold.

Barry's third album offered a fuller refinement of his expanded musical scope. The City Rhythm Band at this point included Alan Axelrod, keyboards; Sid McGinnis, guitar; Steve Donaghey, bass; and Lee Gurst, drums and percussion. Barry's backup trio billed at this point as the Flashy Ladies (which later evolved into Lady Flash), included Debra Byrd, Ramona Brooks, and Reperata (Lorraine Mazzola).

Barry with Linda Allen. *Photo by Irv Steinberg - Globe Photos*

In addition to Bruce Johnson's "I Write the Songs," the album's tracks include Larry Wess's "Lay Me Down," and Phil Galdston and Peter Thom's

"Why Don't We Live Together." The title cut "Tryin' to Get the Feeling," was penned by singer/songwriter David Pomerantz. Barry's music fills the rest of the album, including "Bandstand Boogie," which is the original "American Bandstand" theme from the Dick Clark TV show.

For the first time since the theme was originally written in the 1940s by Les and Larry Elgart, Barry Manilow and Bruce Sussman gave it lyrics. "It never had lyrics," Barry has said, "I researched it and I found out that there were never any lyrics put to it. . . . I called Dick Clark and he sent me the original version. So I copied the old 'Big Band' thing. We put lyrics to it, note for note, even the old saxophone solo; we put lyrics to that part too. And I did my little thirty-two voices on it, and it's really fun! It came out great!"

"It's just an overdub," Barry explained of how one vocalist is able to do thirty-two tracks in rhythmic synchronization. "The tape is big, and it's divided into sixteen different tracks. You record one on top of the other, and as you record, then you play back what you record and harmonize to it. Then you play back both of those, and harmonize to that ... and then you just keep playing it. That's why it says thirty-two vocals, which means there's thirty-two separate vocals, but I'm harmonizing to most of them. It's not like I was singing the same thing. It's all harmonies, and all background stuff."

Barry had used the same "overdubbing" technique on "Cloudburst" in the *Barry Manilow I* album, and on "Avenue C" in the *Barry Manilow II* album.

During the fall of 1975, Barry did a three-month tour which included an engagement with Helen Reddy at the MGM Grand Hotel in Las Vegas. The tour ended New Year's Eve at the Beacon Theater in New York City.

The Beacon Theater performance was given in association with Hospital

Audience, Inc., which had arranged for 2,000 institutionalized and disadvantaged individuals from orphanages, drug programs, schools for the emotionally disturbed and retarded, and senior citizen centers to attend the show without charge. The performance was not open to the general public.

At a press conference held on December 31, 1975, Barry said, "I've always wanted to do a free concert. This year has been fantastic for me and since my success has come from pop AM radio, I figured the audience who would get off most on what I do would be an AM audience, older folks and kids."

Yes, 1975 had been a good year for Barry. He sold over 4 million single records and over 1.6 million albums that year! He had been declared Top New Male Vocalist for Albums and Singles by *Record World* and *Cashbox*. *Music Retailer* dubbed him Top New Male Artist and *Radio & Records* gave him its Pop Artist of the Year award.

"Mandy" was included in the 1975 Grammy Award nominations.

After the eighteenth Annual Grammy Awards presentation in February 1976 declared The Captain and Tennille's "Love Will Keep Us Together," to be the Record of the Year, Barry said, "The Grammy this year? They should have photographed my legs shaking. That audience—it was like performing at Sam Goody's. I was looking out at all the album covers I'd ever seen in my life. If 'Mandy' had won, it would have been a surprise to me. 'Love Will Keep Us Together' was in fact the biggest record of the year."

In the bicentennial year, Barry's new couple of projects were released to the public in a steady flow. In March, the single "Tryin' to Get the Feeling" came out, and by May was in the top ten. The Lady Flash debut album on RSO Records *Beauties In The Night*, was released that summer along with the single "Street Singin'," which quickly made its way to the top forty.

Barry chats with Shirley MacLaine. *Photo by Irv Steinberg · Globe Photos*

Produced by Barry and Ron Dante at Media Sound Studios, Manilow wrote half of the tunes with help from his usual bank of lyricists.

In July Arista Records released Barry's fourth album, *This One's For You*. The immediate demand for the disc was so overwhelming that it *shipped* gold; that is, there were already orders for the first 500,000 copies of the album before they left the warehouse. Within a short time it had become Barry's third platinum L.P.!

That same month, Barry and his entourage left on a ninety-eight-city tour that would last nine months! Lee Gurst recalls what went into such a vast undertaking: "Blood, sweat, and tears; craziness and insanity and nerves—a lot of things! You take on something like that . . . and it's pretty heavy! The show that you put together—it doesn't make any difference whether you put it together for ninety-eight cities, or ninety-eight countries, or ninety-eight months—you do the same quality of show for one audience. . . . So, we spent . . . I think, about four weeks in rehearsals; by the time you include vocal rehearsals, music rehearsals, dance rehearsals, final rehearsals. You put it all together for a week or two, and then you take it on tour, and then you rehearse it some more to polish up the things that you begin to discover once it actually works in front of an audience. . . .

"This last ninety-eight-city thing . . . it was long. It dragged on for about nine months! But toward the end it lightened up a little bit. That was the most difficult of tours, because Barry Manilow was becoming something much bigger than he had ever started out. That put a lot of pressure on him. He couldn't just go out and eat after a show, and he couldn't just go for a walk in a shopping center if he wanted to. He didn't have the freedom he did before. When you lose that freedom, you begin to feel the pressure of the fans . . . and being well-known and recognizable. It's hard to adjust to.

"Your personal life has to go through an adjustment; you don't have the freedom to go out, like I said. There's no choice but to stay in the hotel, when you'd rather be out shopping for shoes and things.

"On the other hand," Lee continued,

"it was an incredibly rewarding tour, because we'd gone to cities where we had never been. It's strange to pull into a city like that, where you've barely heard the name of the city . . . or you've never even seen it, and the people yelling and screaming at you as though you were an old friend. That was incredibly satisfying."

Before the tour had even ended, the single version of "This One's for You" was strongly lodged in the top twenty, just two months after its release. Its successor, "Weekend in New England," by Richard Kerr and Will Jennings, began its rise up the charts.

Barry's fourth album, *This One's For You*, contains nine Manilow originals. Lady Flash handled the background vocals, Manilow played piano and sang, Steven Donaghey played bass, Alan Axelrod did additional keyboards, and Lee Gurst was on drums. Lee is also responsible for the front and back album cover photos on this album, as well as the back cover shot of Barry and his beagle, Bagel, on the *Tryin' To Get The Feeling* album.

In planning the ninety-eight-city tour, two weeks were set aside for a holiday spectacular at the Uris Theater on Broadway. From December 21, 1976, through January 2, 1977, Barry and his touring family did their thing for standing-room-only audiences in the 1,900-seat theater.

The song "It's Just Another New Year's Eve," was written especially for the holiday show. Barry has explained how it came to be: "All during the two weeks that we were preparing for the New Year's Eve show, I was thinking to myself, 'What can I do for these people who come to see me on New Year's Eve other than just dropping balloons and passing out champagne?' I really don't know anyone who really looks forward to that one night. So, me and Marty Panzer sat down and wrote this tune with that in mind. And, this one's for our generation you know . . . because I don't know what 'Auld Lang Syne' means anyway! What does it mean? So, this one's for us."

The week of February 26, 1977, Barry's single version of "Weekend in New England" was in the top ten and on March 2, the first "Barry Manilow TV Special" was broadcast on ABC-TV. The show was aired on a Wednesday evening at 10:00 p.m. and the Neilsen Ratings estimated 35 million viewers watched on their small screens! The one-hour variety special mainly featured Barry's music and his guests were Lady Flash and Penny Marshall of the TV series "Laverne and Shirley."

Variety, the show business weekly newspaper, reviewed "The Barry Manilow Special" in glowing terms. The review noted how difficult it is for rock recording stars to make the transition to TV special productions because the style, discipline, focus, and audience are so different. The review also stated that Barry did "better than most, primarily because his choice of material and his basic musicianship is better and more sophisticated than most of his peers in the pop music field." That obviously is part of the key to Barry's widespread musical appeal.

As a direct result of his television exposure, *Barry Manilow I* and *Barry Manilow II* reentered the *Billboard* charts the weeks of March 12 and 19, respectively.

The monster-size tour wound up with a two-week engagement at the MGM Grand Hotel in Las Vegas on April 13. Barry and all of his backup performers professionally parted ways. Manilow took off for Los Angeles for the summer to work on his fifth studio-produced album, and to start planning for his second TV special. Lady Flash also headed west to plan their second album.

Way back in the spring of 1974 when Barry was putting together his first solo act, he hired Bette Midler's Harlettes as his backup vocal trio. "I had them for my first tour because they

Barry with Reparata, one of the members of his back-up group, Lady Flash. *Photo by Art Zelin - Globe Photos*

were out of work," Barry has said, "and I knew them, and they still knew my material. So I took them along with me, but when I came back from my first six months on the road, I decided I would

With Dick Cavett and Bette Davis. *Photo by Frank Teti*

get my own girls, because it wasn't my
girls, it was Bette's Harlettes. . . . So, I
hired three different girls, and it's good!
I love the Harlettes, they are all my
friends, and they went back to work for

Bette, and everybody's happy now."

As the result of an ad in *Backstage* magazine that read "Manilow Needs Girls," Barry hired Ramona Brooks, Reparata (Lorraine Mazzola), and Debra Byrd. These very individual performers became Barry's Flashy Ladies. Then, in August 1975 Ramona had to leave the group because of problems with her throat. She was replaced by Monica Burruss and the group's name was changed to Lady Flash.

Lady Flash continued as Barry's backup vocal group through April 1977, the end of the ninety-eight-city tour, at which time Barry, his band City Rhythm, and Lady Flash all went their separate ways.

As Lee Gurst has said of Lady Flash: "Barry got them started on their recording career, and the choice is to have them stay a backup group that maybe puts out records now and then, or follow through and become a recording group. And, that means not being a backup group anymore. That means taking a step out front and saying 'We're going to take our shot.' "

Released at the end of April, the single "Looks Like We Made It" from the studio-produced album, *This One's For You*, entered the record charts the first week in May, the same month the deluxe double-album *Barry Manilow Live* was released. Barry's fifth album includes live versions of all of his hit singles up to and including "Looks Like We Made It," as well as the first recorded version of his "Very Strange Medley," and "It's Just Another New Year's Eve."

From May 28 through July 16 all five of Barry's existing albums were on the *Billboard* charts together! *Barry Manilow Live* was number one the week of July 16 and had been certified platinum—Barry's fourth! The following week "Looks Like We Made It" became Barry's third number one single, joining "Mandy" and "I Write the Songs" on his growing list.

Barry best explains the contents of his first double-album, *Barry Manilow Live*: "These discs were recorded live at the Uris Theater in New York City in December 1976, while in the middle of a ninety-eight-city American tour that began in July 1976 and ended in April 1977.

"We have tried to capture some of the incredible excitement with which we were greeted during those ten months, but it was absolutely impossible to even try to capture other equally incredible moments like that show in Chicago when I took off my jacket with a flourish, and my fly was open; that night in Ohio when I ripped Reparata's cape off and it caught on her choker (darn near threw her into the drums before I realized the cape was caught!!); the show when the harp player wouldn't stop playing the last run on 'Weekend in New England' and kept playing all the while I was introducing the next song; that night in Philly when that very strange gentleman jumped up on stage and insisted that he do his imitation of a frog for the entire audience (and he did!!!).

"Hysterically funny moments and infuriatingly maddening moments; the lousy hotels and the spectacular ones, the planes that were late, the food that was gross, the colds, the flu, the broken bones, and all the show business clichés you've ever heard of.

"But miraculously we have all lived to tell the tale and hopefully some of the miracle is on these records."

5

Shine On Bright Star

Barry Manilow rarely talks about the personal side of his life. When the subject of personal relationships comes up, Barry refers to his girl friend and constant companion, Linda Allen, whom he's known since his days in the CBS mailroom. "When I want to have fun, I see Linda. Linda's my lady. We play backgammon together, it's relaxing."

On one occasion Barry declared: "I'm a very private person. I don't want to share my life with anybody!" At another time, in another mood, Barry professed, "Anybody who really needs to, can get to me." Barry's personality would appear to be as multifaceted as his talent.

Although he's reluctant to talk about his personal life, Barry is always willing to discuss his music and his career.

"I'm up from nowhere—Brooklyn—up from nothing. I've worked hard to get here, and I'm gonna work hard to stay here. I can't sleep at night for the music going round in my head.

"I would be doing this no matter what. I didn't care about being successful when I first started out, it never entered my mind. All that concerned me was the need to express myself musically. I had to do it . . . for myself. I would never advise anyone to pursue a career in music unless he or she had something to say. You can't do it for the sake of getting audiences to love you—an ego trip. You've got to do it for yourself. It's either 'art' or 'heart'—as the saying goes. It's so hard. I knew I had to pursue my music, and I had to throw my whole self into it."

Having done that, how does Barry now look upon his role as a starring performer?

"I still consider it a job," he claims, "because of those many years of being in the background and having to be very solid—the brick, the guy that put it all together. Because of all that discipline, I find it easier to do what I have to do, instead of being the freaked-out artist. I know how to deal with musicians and agents and the public as well. If I were a guitar player they found on the street and made into a star, I might not know how to handle it all."

Barry's devotion and attention are directed to his music. "My music is well thought out—adult, professional tunes. All I'm really trying to do is bring back intelligent music. I haven't figured out my 'style' yet, and sometimes I wonder if I really do have a 'style.' But I'm on to something that a lot of people are getting off on!"

There can be no doubt but that Barry Manilow plans to be around for a long while and that he is continually seeking new avenues for his talents. "I was thinking of doing a film score if I could get one. Somebody offered me a theme for a television show which I'm not very sure I want to do. I would like to do a real nice film score, though. I'd like to get my teeth into something like that. The performing is really fun, and I enjoy doing it. I'm glad everybody likes it. I like it, too."

In addition to composing a musical score for a film, Barry has also thought about doing a little acting. "I'm very strongly considering acting in movies. I could be a terrible actor for all I know. I probably *will* turn out to be a terrible actor—but I'm sure gonna try. I had never sung before; I had never performed in front of an audience before; but I've certainly become a very hot draw, haven't I? I guess that this is the time for me to make my move . . . take some risks."

Don Kirshner has more confidence in Barry's acting potential than Barry has: "I think Barry, because of the way he looks, and his sensitivity... he could play a psychopathic killer, and it would be great; or he could play a gentleman, and it would be great; or he could play the kid who is a rebel like in *Easy Rider*. It has to be the right part, but anything can happen with the right vehicle. He obviously is bright, he's got a lot of stage presence, he knows how to handle people, he's paid his dues; so I think he can make it.

"Certainly, if you put him on Broadway tomorrow," Don continues, "he would probably be a giant with the right script, or the right part! That's really the excitement of this business, to sit and see a kid come in and play the piano... and the next time you see him, he's the biggest star in the country! It's very, very exciting!"

And Barry's friend Lee Gurst can also foresee a time when Barry will become an actor. "Well, films are a natural. Films loom on the horizon as something new and challenging. I think everybody likes to find new challenges. Television continues . . . that won't be new. The shows hopefully will be new and creative. To do another recording would not be new. To do another television show will not be new, even though it may be a new type of television show. Films are a new area. Barry has retained his roots and his love for the theater, and I'm sure would like very much to be involved in a Broadway show. Composing a Broadway show—maybe even performing in a Broadway show. I don't know."

It's interesting that not one of Barry's friends even considers the possibility that he will rest on his well-earned laurels. Of course, Barry has made enough money for him to live comfortably for the rest of his life. But Barry Manilow not working is just unthinkable!

"Barry as an artist . . . Barry as a person . . . is very talented, a little bit

The music master in action! *Photos by Nate Cutler - Globe Photos*

restless, very creative, and will be looking for new avenues to express himself," Lee has said. "So, it will be natural for him to go very purposefully into other areas. I think films, Broadway, things like that, will be happening sooner than, say, five years. There are opportunities waiting to be found. Barry's thinking in those directions and when the opportunities present themselves—or can be created—he'll be there."

Because of his firm commitment to his music, Barry Manilow will probably continue to write, arrange, and perform his own compositions. Television specials, recordings, and tours are great vehicles for him. It is unlikely that he will cast aside these opportunities as he pursues new ones. Is there any chance Barry will ever work with Bette Midler again?

"I'm her friend, you know . . . we hang out together. But I'm really not involved in that part of her life anymore," Barry claims. "Eventually, I'm sure we'll get back together again. But, I mean . . . there's just no time. Frankly, I'd love to go back and get it out for her; to go back on the road with her would be a lot of laughs. But there's just no time. Me, thinking about our going out together, man, that's just crazy!"

Barry Manilow is now in a position where he can set his own goals, decide exactly what he wants to do, and when he will do it. If he thinks at all like Irv Biegel, then the sky is no limit for his extraordinary musical talent.

"I think Barry will be the male Barbra Streisand!" Irv has said. "I believe it! I think Barbra Streisand is the biggest star in our business—all aspects of the business—because our business is so intertwined today with film and television, and people crossing over.

"I mean there are a lot of good performers, but when you talk about a

Streisand, and you talk about a Sinatra
. . . I think Barry Manilow can reach
that sphere."

Irv Biegel was right when he signed
Barry to that first record contract, and
he may well be right in his predictions
as to what the future holds for the
shining star that is *Barry Manilow*:

"I can see this thing lasting . . . not
forever, nothing lasts forever. But as
far as being a performer and establishing himself, this man's going to be
around for the next twenty-five years!
And he'll get better. As good as he is,
he's going to get better, because he's
matured."

Friends and followers alike look
with great expectation to a future filled
with beautiful music written, sung, and
played by this very special guy from
Brooklyn.